Published in the UK in 2022 by White Daisy Press

Copyright © H.J.Gilfrew 2022

H.J.Gilfrew has asserted his right under the
Copyright, Designs and Patents Act, 1988, to be identified
as the author of this work.

All rights reserved. No part of this book may be reproduced, stored in a retrieved system or transmitted, in any form or by any means, electronic, mechanical, scanning, photocopying, recording or otherwise, without the prior permission of the author and publisher.

This book is a work of fiction, and except in the case of historical or geographical fact, any resemblance to names, place and characters, living or dead, is purely coincidental.

Paperback ISBN: 978-1-7396032-0-5

Cover design and typeset by SpiffingCovers

DAISY
GOES FOR TEA WITH MRS C.

H. J. GILFREW

To Mrs C.
"Because you believed in me, I also believed."

One pleasant sunny afternoon, Mum and Daisy set off for walkies. "Where are we going today?" Daisy asked excitedly.

Mum replied, "We've had a special invitation to have tea with Mrs C., our elderly neighbour."

"Excellent," said Daisy, already picturing tall cakes, cream buns and lots of chocolate as she walked alongside Mum.

Daisy checked out everything along the way,
then Mum unexpectedly stopped and happily said, "Here we are!"

Daisy looked around.

In front of her was a grand house tucked behind
graceful shrubberies, hedges and trees.

She noticed tall trees and heard birds singing high in the branches.

Then appeared a little bird with a red breast. Flying past Daisy, the bird landed on some black pots full of daffodils leading up to a rather large door surrounded by ivy.

"Hello there," the tiny shape said. Daisy stared back at the rather weird, feathered creature before her. "I'm Mr Robin."

But before Daisy could utter a word, Robin said, "Are you here for tea? So you know, I get to eat all the leftover cakes and cream buns."

"I guess so," said Daisy, looking up at Mum as she pushed her finger into the ivy, touching an odd-looking shape on the wall that made a noise.

DING DONG, DING DONG.

The sound reached Daisy's ears.

Eek! Daisy thought. *That's loud.*

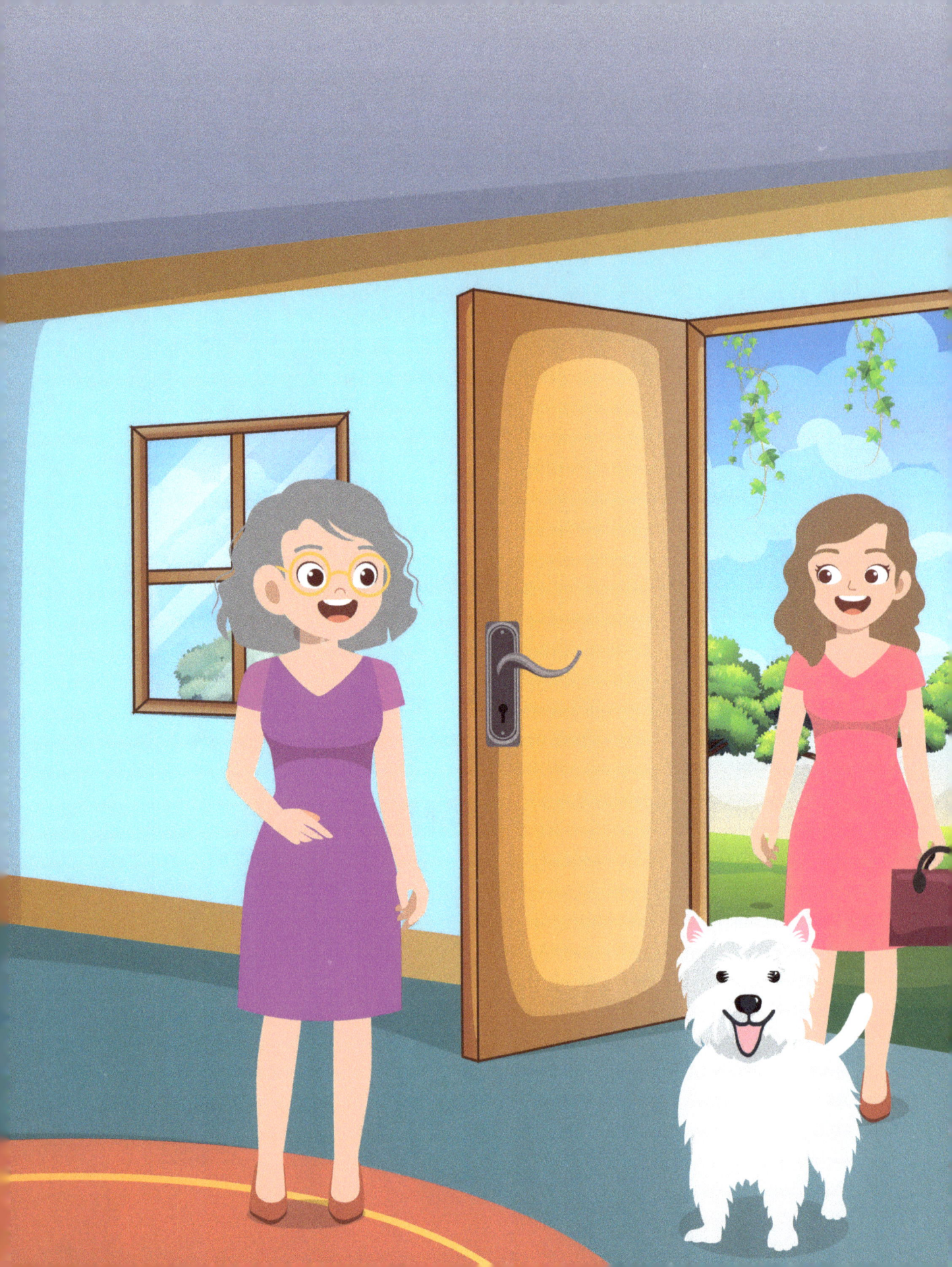

Mum stepped back a little, then the door opened wide with a bit of a creak. There stood a smartly dressed woman in fine linen with gold-framed glasses and short wavy, silver hair.
"Good afternoon, Mrs C.," Mum said.

"Good afternoon, do come in," said Mrs C.
"You are very welcome, you too, Daisy."

Weird, she knows my name, Daisy thought, looking puzzled. She strolled in through the front door looking all around, expecting Mr Robin to follow.

"See you later, Daisy," said Mr Robin as he flew off. "Keep some crumbs for me. I'll be back later, Daisy."

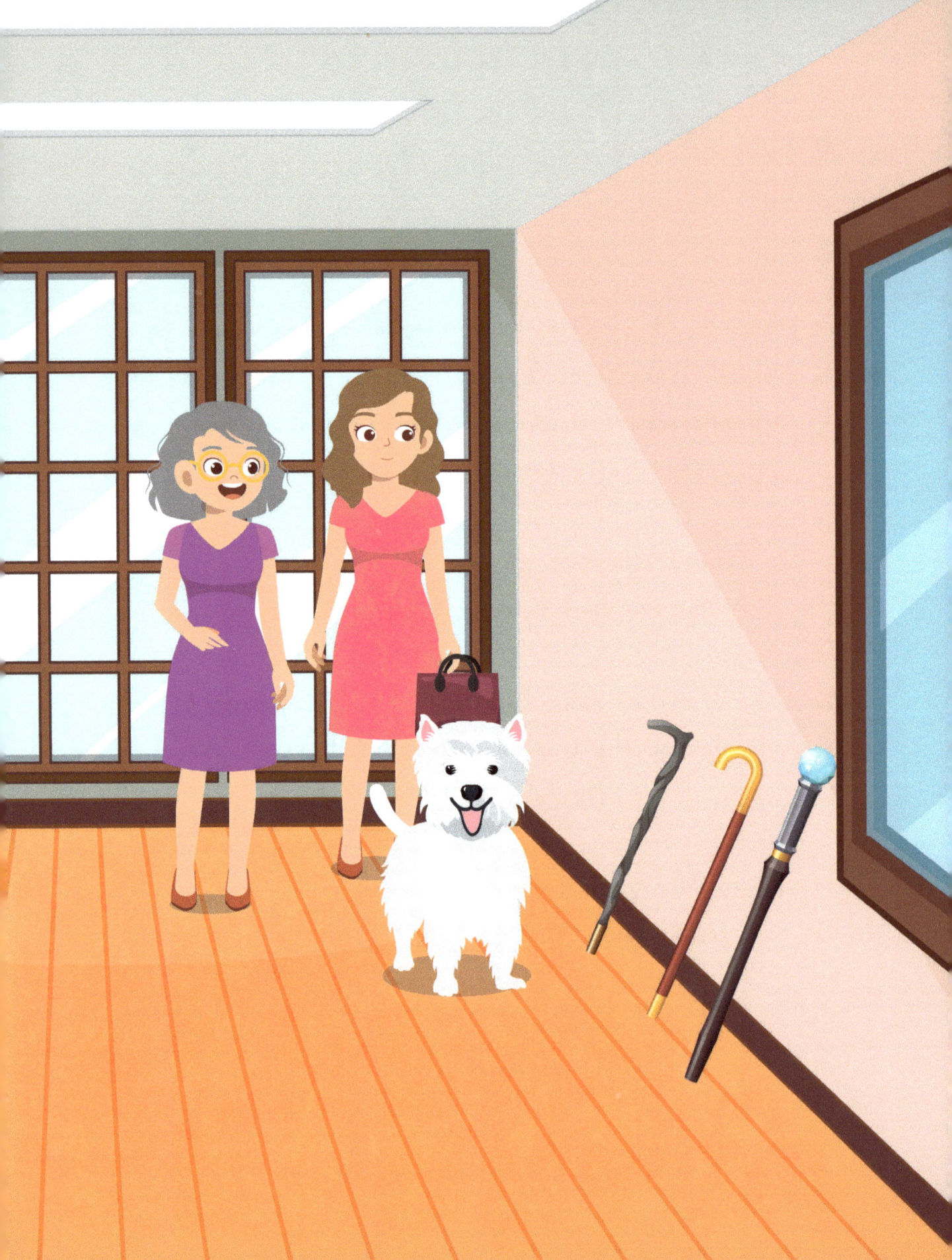

As she continued making her way alongside Mum, having a good old sniff and a nosey up the hallway, she noticed some walking sticks and a very long large mirror.

How handsome, she thought, moving from side to side.

Mrs C. noticed Daisy admiring herself and said, "You're so pretty."

Daisy glanced over and saw Mrs C. admiring her in the mirror, all shy and wagging her tail. Daisy turned to Mum for approval.

"Just beautiful," said Mum. "Isn't she so, so cute, now?"

"Follow me," said Mrs C., smiling as she opened up a large glass door and led them up another step.

From there, they walked into a beautiful kitchen, and the fresh smell of homemade bread and jam lingered out onto another narrow hallway.

Mrs C. opened another glass door and said with a big smile, "Welcome, this is the conservatory. Come and sit around the table, we're all set for tea. I'll finish boiling the kettle. Make yourself comfortable. I'll be back in a few minutes."

Daisy hopped up onto the chair, looking around the table with excitement. The table was set traditionally with a giant teapot. Mum and Daisy enjoyed a beautiful view of the incredible display of flowers from Mrs C.'s garden.

Then, just as she had imagined there was everything you'd need for a particular tea party. In came Mrs C. with trays of sandwiches and a cake stand overflowing with tall cakes, cream buns and lots of chocolate. Daisy's mouth melted.

"I have an extra special treat for Daisy," said Mrs C.

For me? thought Daisy, *what about...?* Then, before she could say anything more, down came a plate before her.

"Yum, that looks nice," said Daisy.

"I ordered this cake especially for you from the doggy bakery," said Mrs C. "Tuck in while I have a good old catch up with your mum."

While Mrs C. and Mum both talked, Daisy looked around the sunny room. She could see a complete description of Mrs C, who she was and her life — this room was all about her family in great detail.

What a beautiful life she has, thought Daisy.

Mum and Mrs C. continued. They laughed and talked about old times. Daisy listened to the two ladies while enjoying the sun's heat through the glass windows. Daisy thought there was so much to see about Mrs C.'s extraordinary life, just in that big room.

The room contained a large, blue, comfortable sofa, paintings, books, family photographs, ornaments, items her children had made when they were younger, and even a sewing machine.

My oh my, so many beautiful things to see, Daisy thought.

Then Daisy heard a noise coming from the sliding glass doors.

Tap tap tap.

There peering in was Mr Robin. Daisy remembered she had promised him some crumbs.

Tap tap tap.

This time, Mrs C. heard it too. Walking over to the sliding door, she opened it and said, "Meet my little friend, Mr Robin. He's a regular at my tea parties." Mr Robin flew over to the little table by the summer seat, waiting for leftovers.

Daisy watched in amazement as Mrs C. lifted some crumbs and placed them on the little bird table.

"See," said Mr Robin, "didn't I tell you? It's beautiful here, and I'm never forgotten." He sang away to himself with great delight.

Daisy turned to look at Mum.

Mum whispered, "What a magical place to visit. Even the birds love her. Isn't this a wonderful place full of love, where everyone is welcome, and everything is cared for, just the way it should be?"

Mrs C. called Daisy and Mum to come to the garden. They both left the table and followed Mrs C. around the patio as she showed them her magnificent display of garden flowers and pots.

You could tell she was proud and attended to them well, watering them with love and attention.

They repaid her love with a delightful display as they danced back and forth, catching every ray of sunshine that peered through the cotton clouds in the blue sky.

Fantastic feeling, thought Daisy.

Mum and Mrs C. continued to chat. Mum listened to her knowledge about caring for plants; she wished she had green fingers like Mrs C.

Daisy, listening in and looking around for Mr Robin, spied him still perched on the bird table watching her.

"Having a good day then?" said Mr Robin, as he flew down to the edge of the path.

"Excellent," said Daisy.

Just then, Mum called to her. "We'll be going soon, fetch your lead."

Daisy sighed to Mr Robin.

"Don't worry," said Mr Robin. "You're part of the family now, Daisy."

"I'm amazed," said Daisy, "about all the lovely things I've learned from this exciting visit. The importance of just calling on someone to say hello has touched me."

"Yes," said Mr Robin. "It's amazing what a day can teach us if we stop to learn and listen."

"We will be on our way now, Daisy," said Mum. "Say goodbye to Mrs C."

Daisy thanked her and wagged her tail as fast as possible.
"Goodbye Mr Robin."

"Goodbye Daisy," Mr Robin said.

They continued into the conservatory, along the narrow hallway through the kitchen, past the large mirror and the walking sticks, to the large front door.

They both turned to Mrs C. at the door. They all hugged.

"It has been wonderful to see you both," said Mrs C, with a big smile.

"Please call again soon."

Daisy's heart, full of love, skipped a beat while walking away that day, all happy, thinking about the exciting stories she had gathered upon her visit to Mrs C. and her beautiful life.

www.ingramcontent.com/pod-product-compliance
Lightning Source LLC
Chambersburg PA
CBHW051321110526
44590CB00031B/4432